Event PATH

Knowing the plan God has for your life through each event

Galen T. Gill

Copyright © 2017 by Galen T. Gill

Event Path
Knowing the plan God has for your life through each event
by Galen T. Gill

Printed in the United States of America.

Edited by Xulon Press.

ISBN 9781629528687

All rights reserved solely by the author. The author guarantees all contents are original and do not infringe upon the legal rights of any other person or work. No part of this book may be reproduced in any form without the permission of the author. The views expressed in this book are not necessarily those of the publisher.

Unless otherwise indicated, Scripture quotations taken from the King James Version (KJV) – *public domain.*

Scripture quotations taken from the New King James Version (NKJV). Copyright © 1982 by Thomas Nelson, Inc. Used by permission. All rights reserved.

Scripture quotations taken from the Holy Bible, New International Version (NIV). Copyright © 1973, 1978, 1984, 2011 by Biblica, Inc.™. Used by permission. All rights reserved.

Scripture quotations taken from the Good News Translation (GNT). Copyright © 1992 American Bible Society. Used by permission. All rights reserved.

www.xulonpress.com

Table of Contents

Introduction vii

Event 2004 9
    – Dad passed away
    – Mom passed away
Event 2005 14
    – The car wreck
Event 2006 16
    – Sister passed away
Event 2007 19
    – The Wedding
    – Grandmother passed away
Event 2008 20
    – The kidney transplant
Event 2013 22
    – Beginning of UOP
Event 2014 24
    – The torn kneecap
    – The torn Achilles
Event 2016 27
    – Diabetes scare
    – Kidney scare
    – The graduation

Acknowledgments 31

Introduction

I have come to realize God has His hand on my life with all the mess ups and wrong decisions I have made. His covering over my life has blocked the seen and unseen disasters that tried to take my life. God's plan was to deliver me from self-hate. The way He moved in my life is amazing. I remember growing up in Detroit, Michigan, my mother would take me to church. At the age of ten, we moved to Nashville, Tennessee and I noticed church was not a part of our life anymore. Yet, still in that small amount of time, there was a willingness to help and to serve others in my spirit.

So, when my mother became sick with cancer in 2000, the second time, it was easy for me to help take care of her. At the beginning, it was easy, but as the cancer spread throughout my mother's body, the challenges of taking care of her became difficult. As a person who worked the night shift, I would get off work at seven a.m., to come home to find my mother getting dressed to go to a job she had in 1980. It was hurtful to tell her that she could not go to work, when she worked so hard all her life.

Then, there was the changes to her body. She often wanted me to rub her back. Her back had knots and sores from where the cancer had taken over. What got me was the effect of the chemotherapy. Not only did she lose her hair, but after so much chemo, her eyes bulged out of their sockets. The first time I saw this, she quickly turned away from me. It scared me. Each day I did not know what to expect when I came home from work.

Soon, I asked my sister (Sheryl) to move in to help watch over our mother and grandmother. By the time my sister moved in, I helped in taking care of not only my mother and grandmother, but also my dad and great aunt. I embraced taking care of my family. The only problem was I lost myself in them. Who am I at this point? I am a soul in search of life.

In 2003, I met my soon to be wife (Julie), at church. As we dated, I did not understand her role in my life. I felt that I had too many issues that I need to address with myself. Would I be able to give her the attention she would like, when taking care of so many people. Something had to give; the one thing I knew was God was in control. Yet, I felt myself wrestling with God for control of my life. I had to go through a series of events before I gave God complete control.

> **Genesis 32:28:** "Then the man said, 'Your name will no longer be Jacob, but Israel, because you have struggled with God and with humans and have overcome.'"

As you can see, after hearing God's voice, my flesh was not willing to change. I was scared to turn over my life to the unknown. With so many questions like, How does this new life work? How do Christians believe in God when things don't go as planned? This is one of my questions as a child in Christ, as I will soon grow up with many challenges.

Event 2004

Prior to the year 2004, God spoke to me in 2000, saying "You need to change." The message came to me on vacation in Daytona, Florida. I thought I was going to Florida to turn up, but God had other plans for me. At a club, I became sick and went back to the hotel. At the hotel, I sat on the balcony as the lighting filled the sky. Looking at the sky, amazed at the light show God provided for me, the message came, "You need to change." Yes, I thought I was going crazy as that was my first time hearing God clearly. Don't get me wrong, He is always talking, I just was not listening.

As Sunday approached, I realized this was my last day seeing the group I was with. I did not want this change, but I felt my spirit crying for more. Not telling anyone about my experience with God, as soon as we got back home, God sent His angel to me, she invited me to church. My flesh was not willing to change, so I gave the angel all kinds of excuses on why I could not go to church. If it was not for that Angel being persistent and on assignment, I easily would have not come to church. My life changed and oh what a change it was. A baby in Christ, who knew, but I wouldn't stay a baby for long.

1 Corinthians 1:30: "But God has brought you into union with Christ Jesus, and God has made Christ to be our wisdom. By him we are put right with God; we become God's holy people and are set free."

As God spoke to me, my life would never be the same. The people I hung around, I would see no more. The places and things I did in the world will dissipate. My mind will become transformed to a godly mind. You may ask what happened to me? I found life in Him. Yet, as I found life, I started to have major challenges in the road ahead that would test my faith, and the joy that I found. For several years, I was the caretaker for my mother, father, grandmother, and a great aunt, taking them to doctor appointments, going to nursing homes to visit, and at the same time help raise my son and daughter. The stresses of life started to take over my life. Here I was, picking up my kids on weekends, trying to do the best that I know as a father, but I was crumbling through the week.

> **Job 14:1:** *"Man that is born of a woman is of few days and full of trouble"*

December 31, 2003 at church during the service, I heard God speak to me a second time. As I sat in church, God said, "This is your season to experience death." A feeling of sadness came over me. The next morning sitting on the porch, I told my sister what God told me. I explained to her we need to get financially, emotionally, and spiritually in a good place because our mother will die this year. As I explained to my sister what God said to me, she looked at me and said, "Gone with all that."

After working all night, I received a call from a sheriff on a Monday morning in May 2004.

"I need to see you; can you meet with me so we can talk?"

"No," I said quickly. *Why would I volunteer to meet a sheriff?*

"Sir, I really need to talk to you in person."

"Whatever you have to say you can say it on the phone."

"This is not our procedure, but your dad was found dead in his apartment."

Silence. As tears started to fill my eyes, I thought, *this can't be, I just saw him on Friday.*

"Sir, are you there?"

"Yes," I said in a quiet choking voice.

"Can you meet me? I'm at who I think is your next of kin."

"Yes, on my way."

By this time, my boss was in front of me, sensing something was wrong. He sat me down so I could get myself together.

I was the first to hear of this news. *I have to let both of my aunties know.* I realized I called Aunt Virginia, who was out of town. I don't recall how the phone call went, but I do know it felt like she was here as soon as we hung up the phone.

As I met the Sheriff at my Aunt Nora's house, I road with him to her job. I walked up to her with this sheriff as she was at the register on her job. I let her know that we need to talk. That look on her face plays often in my mind. That looks of fear, as to say what now? The look was as if she said, "Boy don't you bring me bad news."

I went home and didn't understand why. I had just spent the Friday before visiting him at home. We had a wonderful day and my dad opened his feelings to me, telling me that when I was born, he became jealous of me because I took his wife (my mother). With kids of my own, I have learned it is important to know when you have a child, it was you before that child. You must make time to keep the love you have for each other and incorporate the love for your child. That Friday evening was the first time I heard my dad say, "I love you." I left feeling like this was the start of something new for us. We were not as close as I would have liked. We did not do the father/son things, like going to games, fishing, or hanging out. So to hear those three words come out of his mouth made me feel at peace with him. Within a couple of days, I found myself sitting at the funeral home watching and learning the business of burying a loved one.

At first, I did not know why I watched my aunties so closely as we sat at the funeral home planning his home-going celebration. The day of the funeral, as we sat on the front row, God gave me a vision of what He said at the beginning of the year. Before the close of the casket, I looked at my dad, looked at my mom, and when I looked back at the casket, I saw my mother in it. That's when it hit me: the season is starting. Fear, anxiety, and anger came over me. Fear that one day I will be parentless. Anxiety because I don't know when the day will come. And anger because I could not understand this type of love God had given me.

A week later, on my way home from work, I got another phone call. this time it was my sister asking me where I was. As I approached the house, my heart started to beat fast as I saw my sister and a lady on the porch. I didn't want to get out of the car in fear of what was about to happen. The nurse told us there was nothing else they could do for our mother, and suggested we put her in hospice. The cancer had won the battle, but God got the victory.

As I tried to get a grip on what was going on, and the fact that I had not grieved the death of my dad, I grew angry with God. My mindset was, *Why are you doing this to me? Here I am studying your Word, trying to live this life out right, and the reward I get is the death of my parents.* My flesh was at an all-out war with God. Three weeks after my dad's funeral, I was back at the funeral home to make arrangements for my mom. I was still mad at God, but now I was also mad at my parents for not taking care of themselves. I felt like their life was cut short because of the decisions they made. From looking at them on the outside, we did not talk about life. I did not know their relationship with God, and this upset me.

As I went through the funeral process again, I found myself shutting down. I continued to ask God, "Why are you doing this to me? Why did you take my family?" As I continued to go to church, the Sunday after my dad's funeral I think I was okay. The Sunday after my mother's funeral was different. I had people that I was close to ask me why I was going to church when God had taken my parents.

> **Job 13:15:** "Though He slay me, yet will I trust Him. Even so, I will defend my own ways before Him."

At the time of that question, I did not know how to answer why I continued to trust in God. My spirit man pulled me to church as a comfort and for guidance, but at the same time to show others that in the midst of sorrow, we as His children have a responsibility to give God praise and glory. Even though I looked like everything was together on the outside, while I continued to show up at church and serve, I found myself depressed, not knowing what direction my life was headed. I was still not sure why Julie was with me. Soon after we broke up, but God did not break up with us, as we remained friends. God would form a situation that will get us back together.

It was several months when I heard God explain to me why He took both my parents from me. I do believe in the months prior to God speaking, I went into depression. No, I did not get help, but I would force myself to go to church and read the Bible. God told me it was not about me. He explained He got my father to a place that his spirit was not of the world, but was at a point of peace. And for my mother, she told me she was tired, so why would He continue to let her be in pain. I was at a situation with God, as He reminded me that He is in control, and there is a bigger picture that I cannot see. I started to feel the loss of my parents was for the glory of God. It was time for me to learn who God wanted me to be in this life.

Event 2005

After Julie and I broke up in the beginning of 2005, I got to that point where I was tired—tired of being sick and tired. Tired of the dating scene, tired of trying to impress women, tired of living, tired of being a dad, tired of being the go-to person for other peoples' problems. I was tired. This point in my life was a good place to be. When you are tired, God will step in, even when you think He is nowhere around. He will use you when you are at that breaking point in life. At that point, I decided to just learn who I was and to try to be a great father to my kids.

For the year of 2005, I did not go on a date until December. As I escorted a friend to a Christmas party, I felt like life was better as my heart was still heavy from the deaths that I had not grieved. I would keep myself busy in order not to grieve. Because in my mind, I thought if I grieve, then they are gone forever. On our way to drop off the young lady, out of nowhere we are hit. On the driver side of my car, from the front fender to the driver door was pushed in. As we climbed out of the car, the paramedics asked if we were okay. I found myself having a panic attack and going into shock. At the hospital, there was a police officer who told me that from the impact of the car I should have serious injuries or be dead. In fact, I walked away with only a minor scratch in my eye. The suit that I had on was a pin stripe suit. The left side of the suit jacket was shredded to pieces. Where the glass hit the suit, it did not hit my skin.

Isaiah 53:5 (NKJV): "But He was wounded for our transgressions, He was bruised for our iniquities; the chastisement for our peace was upon Him, And by His stripes we are healed."

As my outer appearance was fine, my spirit man questioned God again. I yelled out, "What do you want with me? Can I not have some fun?" As I tried to regain some form of life, I realized I needed my friend back in my life. God placed in my heart that this is the woman He will use in my life for His glory.

I called Julie to see if she could pick me up for the 2005 New Year's Eve service. As we set in the sanctuary, I explained to her that I didn't know what I was doing,. I needed her help to get me though this hell. If it were me, knowing there is a spirit of death over me, I would have run as far as I could away from me. Yet, God showed her something in me. We put all our issues, pain, hurt, and expectations on the line, along with any health issues, financial goals, and spiritual beliefs. Now we knew who each other were and where we would like to see this relationship go. Did we line up with God's plan for us? Was the spirit of death over in my life? At this point, I prayed life would get a little easier. God placed this woman in my life for a reason, and in this season of my life. Not knowing what the future held for us, she gave me another chance.

Event 2006

As I continued to try to get my life right, on a Friday evening while working at my church, I received that frightening call. The call this time came from my stepfather telling me that my sister had died in her apartment. I lost it. I ran out of the church and then fell to the ground in tears. This death hurt me more than my parents because we had so much fun as kids. She was my personal life coach because I was shy and withdrawn from people. I was always made to go with her and her friends, even though most times, I sat in the car. It bothers me because we did not get a chance to resolve our differences on our mother's death, but we knew we loved each other.

After our mother died, we did not talk for a long time. Our relationship became distant without knowing or taking the first step to reconcile. I was left with no immediate family members. My thoughts were, *Will I ever see some type of good in my life again?* I started to question my reason for living. Yes, suicide was on my mind. I was not thinking of my kids, my girlfriend (Julie, at this time in my life), or other people who cared for me. Yet, my pride as a man told me men don't get help or see a psychiatrist. Instead, we bottle everything up on the inside and try to handle the pain and hurt on our own.

This action that I made was dangerous, not only to me, but to my ten-year-old son (Dylan), nine-year-old son (Dominique), six-year-old daughter (Tone'), and other kids who watched my every step. I realized this when

I told Dylan he did not have to come to my sister's funeral. This was just too many funerals for a kid, and this was just on my side of the family. His response to me was, "I need to be there for you." All this time, I thought about me and my feelings as this child looked at my every action with each situation. So, if I was to take the punk way out of life, the message that I would have given him would be to end it when times get hard. That is not the answer. I prayed, and prayed, and prayed God would see me through this dark time. I started to feel like Job in the Bible where God lowered the hedge around him so He could show the devil that even if Job lost it all, he would still give God the praise and glory. That is where I was, but then I remembered the vision in 2004.

God said, "This is your season to experience death."

I realized my season is not God's season.

Psalm 30:5: *"Weeping may endure for a night, but, joy comes in the morning."*

At this point, I had been weeping for two years in this season. I tried to stay strong on this word that the joy was coming. I would see some glimpses of joy here and there, but the total joy that I wanted, I could not find. You may look at me and say joy is in God, but my flesh wanted my mother, father, and sister. The battle between my flesh and spirit was so real. I learned how to stay busy just to keep the thoughts away. I would cry while driving to or from work. I constantly fed my spirit with gospel music and sermons from pastors like Bishop Joseph Walker III, Bishop Paul Morton, and Bishop T.D. Jakes. I did not know who to turn to, because I never experienced this before. Yes, I could have gone to my pastor, and/or counseling, but, I could not explain my emotions of being happy one minute, and sad the next minute. However, what I did do was call on Jesus. Psalm 86:1-4 became my favorite passage in the Bible.

Psalm 86:1-4 (NIV): "Hear me, Lord, and answer me, for I am poor and needy. Guard my life, for I am faithful to you; save your servant who trusts in you. You are my God; have mercy on me, Lord, for I call to you all day long. Bring joy to your servant, Lord, for I put my trust in you."

Mediating on this scripture day and night, knowing He put His trust in me to give Him glory going through each test. I was able to pull myself out of depression, only because He is a God who is in control.

By this time, I thought I was ready to ask the question to Julie. First there was an order that I had to follow. I first talked to her mom (Ms. Sara). I called her to see if I could come and talk to her. Once I got to her place, I started to get nervous.

I knocked on the door, she opened and said, "Yes?"

I told her I had to ask her something. We sat on the couch as my hands started to sweat, and I asked, "I would like to ask Julie to marry me."

She said, "You know she likes to travel, and she is spoiled."

"Yes ma'am, I know."

She said, "Well if you can handle that, you got my blessing, and she comes with a mother

That was my first person to ask. Now I had three kids to convince we will make a good family. My next person was my oldest son, Dylan. I asked him, "I'm going to ask Julie to marry me. What do you think?"

His reply was a typical boy answer. It was, "Okay."

I asked Dominique the same question. He replied, so you will be with us all the time. Yes. That's cool

Then there is my daughter, Tone'. With the same question she replies, don't forget about me. I told her never will I forget about you.

Guess what, my joy is coming, and my smile is for real. She said yes and we are getting married.

Event 2007

Before my joy came, I had to experience one more death: my grandmother, the rock of the family. We had so many good times that I cherished. By this time, I believe I became numb to death. I consciously told myself death is a part of life. Yes, it is hard, but you must press on.

That's right, Julie became my wife in 2007. My joy that I sought was here: a family unit that is an amazing blended family. As we engaged in our premarital sessions, the couple separated us on the last day. The male counselor told me to read and understand Ephesians 5:25, that every man has a test that will relate to this Scripture.

> Ephesians 5:25 (NKJV): *"Husbands, love your wives, just as Christ also loved the church and gave Himself for her."*

I keep this scripture in my wallet and on my computer as a screensaver. As I mentioned, we put everything on the table about ourselves. So, I knew about my wife's health condition; I just did not think we would face it so soon in our marriage.

Event 2008

In the summer of 2008, my wife's health condition grew progressively worse. Her doctor made the decision to place her on the kidney transplant list in July 2008, after my father died of a heart attack and three weeks later, my mother died of cancer in 2004. Then my sister passed in 2006 and my grandmother in 2007. Now facing an uncertain future with my wife, I began to question God. Why did He give me a Grammy that had a crack on the inside—one I could not fix?

I prayed God would see us through this test. After several prayers, I heard from God. I am to test to see if I can become the donor. Throughout the testing, I questioned myself: *Am I going to be able to do this? What if something happens?* With all the questions in my head, I remembered that Scripture I had in my wallet (Ephesians 5:25). I could hear God asking, "What are you willing to give up for your wife? Can you be the husband I called you to be?"

I started putting myself in the Scripture: "Galen, love Julie as Christ loves you, and gave Himself for you." At this point, I learned the church is not a location. The church is in me and wherever I am, He is.

In August 2008, we received the news that we are a perfect match. The surgery was scheduled in November 2008, but it was delayed because additional testing was needed. We knew a delay was not a denial. God, being true to His Word, the surgery took place in December 2008. One week after we were released, my wife had a setback. Her blood had formed a mass around the kidney. I continued to stand on God's Word and pray these two prayers.

> **Isaiah 53:5 (NKJV):** "But He was wounded for our transgressions, He was bruised for our iniquities; the chastisement for our peace was upon Him, and by His stripes we are healed."

> **Psalm 102:1-2 (NKJV):** "Hear my prayer, O Lord, And let my cry come to You. Do not hide Your face from me in the day of my trouble; Incline Your ear to me; In the day that I call, answer me speedily."

As I prayed these Scriptures in the hospital, I stepped out of the room and just a few feet away, there was a nurse reading her Bible. I knew right then that God was in the building, and everything would be all right. This setback was all for a setup in our life. God put us together for His glory. The experience took us to another level of faith, prayer, and worship. I can truly say my wife is a gift from God.

Event 2013

It had been five years with nothing major going on. The family was good; kids were about to graduate and enter college. Life felt good at that point. But, there is so much more that needed to be done.

> **Matthew 9:35-38 (NKJV):** *Then Jesus went about all the cities and villages, teaching in their synagogues, preaching the gospel of the kingdom, and healing every sickness and every disease among the people.-But when He saw the multitudes, He was moved with compassion for them, because they were weary and scattered, like sheep having no shepherd. Then He said to His disciples, "The harvest truly is plentiful, but the laborers are few. Therefore pray the Lord of the harvest to send out laborers into His harvest.*

I thought serving in ministry was enough, but God wants us to go outside the walls of the church. This allows us to reach those who only watch our actions. As death took over my life for some years, I realized it was time for me to do me. I enrolled back into college in August 2013 to better my life and seek more knowledge of my career path. What I thought would be a simple path, God had more in store for me. I was called to help and serve others. God called me to become a deacon. I started the training

September 2013. So I was in two schools at the same time, but God would not put more on me than I can bear.

> **Philippians 1:6 (NKJV)**:*"Being confident of this very thing, that He who has begun a good work in you will complete it until the day of Jesus Christ."*
>
> **Romans 8:30 (NKJV):** *"Moreover whom He predestined, these He also called; whom He called, these He also justified; and whom He justified, these He also glorified."*

When I read scriptures like Philippians 1 and Romans 8, I am encouraged to press my way through any challenge. And the challenges started to come.

Event 2014

The summer of 2014, my wife went on a trip with her girls to Panama, Florida. I had the house to myself, so I thought, *I'm going to eat what I want, sleep, and do nothing until the last day when she is expected back.* I was on my way to work when I received a phone call from my wonderful wife.

"Hey babe!" she said cheerily.

"Hey, you all having fun?"

"Well, I think I messed up."

"Messed up what?"

"I think I messed my knee up."

"You'll be okay," I said, slightly relieved. Her knee moved sometimes, so I did not think much about it. Not to mention she did not sound like she was in any pain.

"No," she said more seriously, "this time my leg is swollen, and I can't bend it."

"Okay, what is going on? Spit it out."

"Well, last night, we went to Coyote Ugly and decided to ride a mechanical bull."

"You did what!"

"Don't get mad at me, but my body went one way and my leg went another way."

"Do I need to come and get you?"

"No, no, no."

"I'm on my way. I can get there six to seven hours."

"No, no, no," she sobbed.

"Did you go to the ER?"

"No."

"So you hurt yourself last night. And have not seen any doctor. Put your friend on the phone," I tried to hide my frustration, but my voice got shakier.

"Hey," said her friend, sounding sad. I am sure she remembered before they left, I told her to take care of my baby.

"This is what I need you to do. Take her to the ER. If there is no ER, take her to a clinic within the next hour. If I don't hear from you within an hour, you let her know I will be there to pick her up."

By that time, I was so mad at everyone there.

All she could say was, "Yes, sir."

So here I was, miles away from my wife, a nervous wreck. When I got the call back from my wife, she told me that she went to a clinic and they wrapped her leg. So now I thought it was not that bad. When she got back home, we went to the doctor's office and get shocking news: her kneecap was on the side of her leg. So we had a major surgery to prepare for.

The surgery went well; there was a lot of therapy. Meanwhile, I had prepared to send my daughter off to college. I was excited for my daughter as we travel down the highway. I did what a father does: unpack, put up, and fix up whatever needed to be done. My wife and I decided not to stay the weekend since the drive was not far.

By the time we made it back home, I got a call from my daughter: "Daddy, I heard something pop in my leg while in training."

That Monday, my daughter found out she tore her Achilles on the first day of practice. Surgery was in her future. Taking care of my wife, traveling up and down the highway to check on my daughter, and in two schools—I did not know the true effects of stress until one day I found myself shaking. My blood pressure was on the rise. The Mayo Clinic suggests stress that is left unchecked can contribute to many health problems, such as high blood pressure, heart disease, obesity, and diabetes. However, I know a doctor who is a healer of all stress, only if you keep your mind on Him.

> **Isaiah 26:3 (KJV):** *"Thou wilt keep him in perfect peace, whose mind is stayed on thee: because he trusteth in thee."*

It is amazing how you can go to church but not have peace. You can fake a smile and be tired of smiling. As I went through the deacon training, I questioned my ability to do this assignment. How can I pray and attend to others, when my house needs a healing and a breakthrough? Each time I felt like this, God would use my pastor to give a word that says, "Don't give up," or "You can't quit." That word given lifted me up to press through any trial. As Christians, we tend to feel like wanting to quit is a weakness in your Christian life. In fact, the flesh is weak, so we need our spirit man to be renewed daily. This is not me, but in fact a Word from God.

> **2 Corinthians 4:16 (KJV):** "For which cause we faint not; but though our outward man perish, yet the inward man is renewed day by day."

Yes, I get tired. Yes, my flesh asks all the questions—what, when, why, and how. But my spirit, based on the Word of God, says I can do, I can have, I can be blessed, and it is okay to feel tired in my flesh. I don't have an option to quit or give up.

Event 2016

In January 2016, I noticed I kept waking up at night to go to the bathroom. This started as one to two times a night, but by mid-January, I was up half the night going to the use the bathroom. My eating habits changed; all I wanted was something cold and sugary. By February 2016, I was at church and noticed I could not see the faces of the choir. *Oh, my gosh! I am going blind.* I said nothing to my wife, until I went to my doctor.

You all know, as men we don't go to the doctor until something falls off. I am so glad I'm not like that anymore. I did wait until it was time for my annual physical. My doctor immediately tested me for diabetes. My count was over 600 and I lost twenty pounds in one month. With only one kidney, my doctor placed me on Insolent and Metformin. She told me, for the first week, I could not eat anything with sugar in it. That meant no coffee, no fruit, no bread, and no pasta. I told her I would not be on this medicine for long. I had to change the way I looked at food and recognize what I put in my body.

This was not an easy process. For over twenty years, I did not eat breakfast. I got up, got my coffee and went with anywhere from one to three Mountain Dews a day, and then eating at night. For twenty years, this was my routine, but now I had to change my mindset when it came to food.

My wife and I grocery shopped together, reading the labels and making sure the total carbohydrates were within my numbers. This was a learning experience for me because I thought the sugar was the important part of the food, but in fact, it is the total carbohydrates.

It was time for my first vacation on this new schedule, and there was food everywhere. The temptation was so real. So, I decide to test myself with my favorite drink. I took my sugar test before and after I drank a Mountain Dew to see the reaction of my sugar. Before, it was 120. After, it was over 300 and this was a canned drink. That day in March was my last time drinking a Mountain Dew.

In the middle of April, I went back for my checkup, confident I would stop the medication that day. My doctor told me she would let me know once the blood work came back. I was a little disappointed, but as we know, a delay is not a denial. A couple of days passed, and I got the call that I can stop taking the insolent. To God be the glory.

In June 2016, she took me off my remaining medication. With exercising and eating right, life will continue. If you do what you can do, God will do the rest.

> **Mark 11:23 (KJV):** "For verily I say unto you, That whosoever shall say unto this mountain, Be thou removed, and be thou cast into the sea; and shall not doubt in his heart, but shall believe that those things which he saith shall come to pass; he shall have whatsoever he saith."

In the midst of battling this disease, another loved one battled cancer. In April 2016, my aunt Nora, and I took a trip to Detroit to see her sister (Virginia). This was the first time in forty years that I spent quality time with Nora. It is amazing how a situation will bring you closer to another relative. It said, "Yes, your aunt in Detroit is dying. But she is not the only aunt that you have. She has a sister that loves you the same or even more than you will think." I thank God for the opportunity and the life of Virginia Hill. I also think God for the chance to laugh and cry with my aunt Nora.

In June 2016, I got my healing and tried to get in the graduation mood, so now the attack turned on my wife. Her kidney, after eight years, started to be rejected by her body. Can you say prayer changes everything? The power of prayer, and believing the prayer will manifest to give God the Glory. With two weeks in the hospital, her spirit inspired not only me, but so many others by giving encouraging words on the situation. She showed me the true meaning of fighting in your spirit and at the same time, show faith in God and total healing will come upon her body. Through all that we have been through, this time was stressful, but at the same time, we have peace that God is able to do above and beyond anything we can imagine.

It was graduation time, why was I not happy? My graduation happened thirteen days after my mother's birthday and one day after my dad's birthday.

When you think about this journey, from 2004 to 2016, it is thirteen years of test after test. Some may say, "You have bad luck," or, "You are cursed with the number thirteen." We associate thirteen with bad luck, but when you look at the number from a spiritual eye, the number thirteen is a blessing from Abraham. He was eighty-six when Ishmael was born and ninety-nine when God spoke the blessing over Abraham. I am so thankful that God do not judge me for me, but provide continue blessing on my life.

> **Genesis 16:15-16 (KJV):** "And Hagar bare Abram a son: and Abram called his son's name, which Hagar bare, Ishmael. And Abram was fourscore and six years old, when Hagar bare Ishmael to Abram."
>
> **Genesis 17 (KJV):** When Abram was ninety-nine years old, the Lord appeared to Abram and said to him, "I *am* Almighty God; walk before Me and be blameless. ² And I will make My covenant between Me and you, and will multiply you exceedingly."

After thirteen years, God placed this book in my spirit to encourage you to put whatever is stressing you out in God's hands. That moment that you want to quit is not an option. If you are an adult, there is a young child you don't know who is watching how you handle that situation. They want to be like you and learn from you. If you quit, what will the impact be on that child? If you are a child or teenager, your future is at hand. Don't let your dreams die with you. Some things will be tough, but find that spirit in you that say, "I am more than conqueror."

> Romans 8:37 (KJV): *"Nay, in all these things we are more than conquerors through him that loved us."*

I can only speak from a male point of view, we have so much in stake on this earth. If we submit to God first, we will be able to take back what the enemy has taken. I have learned God will see me through, even when I think my flesh can't handle another thing.

> Deuteronomy 30:5-6 (KJV): And the LORD thy God will bring thee into the land which thy fathers possessed, and thou shalt possess it; and he will do thee good, and multiply thee above thy fathers. And the LORD thy God will circumcise thine heart, and the heart of thy seed, to love the LORD thy God with all thine heart, and with all thy soul, that thou mayest live.

My prayer as you read my story is that you will see your story and share it with others. God does not want us to go through a test and be silent. The test is for that brother, sister, friend, peer, and co-worker who may be going through a similar experience and doesn't know which way to turn, but when they see you going through it with your head up, giving God all the praise.

Acknowledgments

I give God all the glory that He trusts me to give Him praise
through the good and bad experiences in my life.

I thank God for my amazing wife, Julie Gill and kids:
Dylan, Dominique, and Tone'.

The family members who are not here with me,
but have placed value in me. May you rest in God's hands.
I love you all.

Marie King (Grandmother), Helen Gill (Mother),
Jimmie Gill (Father), Sheryl Coffee (Sister),
and Virginia Hill (Aunt).

References

http://www.mayoclinic.org/healthy-lifestyle/stress-management/in-depth/stress-symptoms/art-20050987

"Stress Symptoms: Effects on Your Body and Behavior." *Mayo Clinic*. N.p., 28 Apr. 2016. Web. 17 Feb. 2017.

www.ingramcontent.com/pod-product-compliance
Lightning Source LLC
LaVergne TN
LVHW021745060526
838200LV00052B/3481